TABLE OF CONTENTS

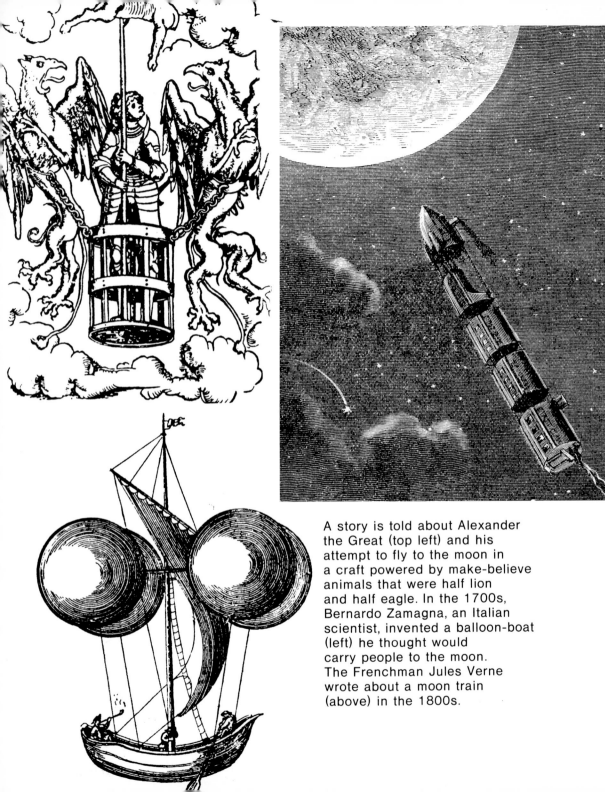

A story is told about Alexander the Great (top left) and his attempt to fly to the moon in a craft powered by make-believe animals that were half lion and half eagle. In the 1700s, Bernardo Zamagna, an Italian scientist, invented a balloon-boat (left) he thought would carry people to the moon. The Frenchman Jules Verne wrote about a moon train (above) in the 1800s.

A New True Book

SPACECRAFT

By Darlene R. Stille

CHILDRENS PRESS®
CHICAGO

Someday, people may build and live in space colonies.

PHOTO CREDITS

AP/Wide World Photos—6 (bottom), 12, 18 (2 photos), 25 (right), 32, 40

© Jerry Hennen—8

Historical Pictures Service—4 (3 photos)

NASA—Cover, 2, 11, 16, 17, 19 (2 photos), 20, 21 (2 photos), 22, 23, 24, 25 (left), 26 (2 photos), 28, 29, 31, 34 (2 photos), 35 (top), 36, 37, 38 (2 photos), 39, 41, 42, 43, 44, 45

James Oberg—13 (right)

Photri—13 (left), 35 (bottom left and right)

Smithsonian, National Air & Space Museum—14

UPI/Bettmann Newsphotos—6 (top left and top right)

COVER: The Magellan spacecraft released into space from the space shuttle *Atlantis*

Library of Congress Cataloging-in-Publication Data

Stille, Darlene R.
    Spacecraft / by Darlene R. Stille.
        p.   cm. — (A New true book)
    Includes index.
    Summary: Describes a variety of spacecraft from past, present, and future, including the early rockets, the space shuttle, and possible space stations.
    ISBN 0-516-01120-0
    1. Space vehicles—Juvenile literature.
[1. Space vehicles.] I. Title.
TL793.S756 1991   90-19992
629.47—dc20   CIP
                                          AC

HOW THE SPACE AGE BEGAN

The Space Age began in 1957, when the Soviet Union sent a small satellite into space.

Long before this, people had dreamed of flying into space. Science-fiction writers wrote stories about people building spacecraft and flying to the Moon and to other planets.

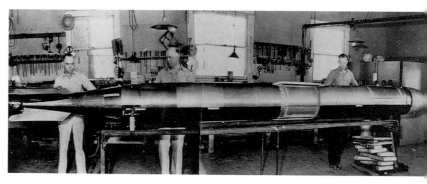

The American Robert H. Goddard (left) is honored as the pioneer of rocket science. One of Goddard's rockets is seen above. The development of space rockets saw many failures. Below, a Vanguard test rocket explodes on takeoff in 1957.

But before this could happen, scientists had to find a way of getting the spacecraft up and away from the pull of Earth's gravity. The only way to do this was to build huge rockets.

THE MAKING OF ROCKETS

A rocket is the most powerful type of engine for its size. It works by burning fuel in a closed space, called a combustion chamber. The burning fuel creates hot gases. These gases expand rapidly and press against the walls of the combustion chamber.

The giant Saturn V rocket carried Apollo spacecraft into space.

There is an opening at the rear of the combustion chamber. When the gas escapes through the opening, the pressure at the rear is reduced.

The pressure at the front
of the rocket stays the same,
and this greater pressure
drives the rocket forward.
This creates the power to
send objects high into the sky.

A Saturn rocket
carrying *Skylab 4*
lifts off the
launch pad.

Rockets probably were invented by the Chinese sometime in the 1200s. Early Chinese rockets were used mainly for carrying fireworks into the sky. Chinese armies also used rockets as weapons. They called them "arrows of flying fire." But these rockets were small and not very powerful.

The more fuel a rocket can hold and burn, the more powerful the rocket is. And

The huge external fuel tank of the Space Shuttle is over 150 feet long and carries more than 1.5 million pounds of fuel.

the bigger a rocket is, the more fuel it can hold.

During the 1800s and early 1900s, bigger and more powerful rockets were invented. They carried bombs and were used as weapons.

During the 1950s, scientists in the United States and the Soviet Union learned how to use powerful rockets to send spacecraft beyond the pull of Earth's gravity.

An *Explorer* satellite was launched on top of a powerful Jupiter rocket.

THE FIRST SPACECRAFT

The first spacecraft was a satellite that orbited Earth. It was launched by the Soviet Union on October 4, 1957. This is the day on which the Space Age officially began. The satellite, called *Sputnik 1*, was carried into space on top of a rocket.

Sputnik 1 (below) looked like a spiked ball. The painting at right shows *Sputnik* being hurled into orbit.

The Soviets launched *Sputnik 2* in November 1957. This spacecraft carried the first living creature into space—a dog named Laika.

The United States sent up its first spacecraft on January 31, 1958. This was a satellite called *Explorer 1*.

Explorer 1, America's first artificial satellite, was launched in 1958.

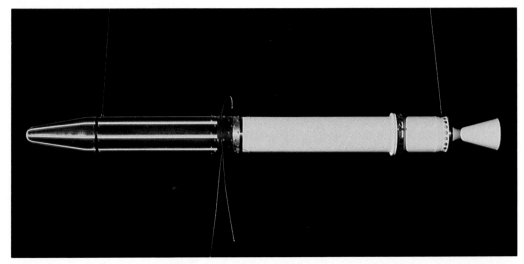

Other small spacecraft were soon launched. Most of these were satellites carrying scientific instruments.

These early spacecraft were used to study what it is like in space. They studied the gases in Earth's upper atmosphere. They studied radiation from deep space.

Spacecraft even landed on the Moon. These early spacecraft helped prepare the way for sending people into space.

BUILDING SPACECRAFT FOR PEOPLE

Soviet cosmonaut Aleksey A. Leonov (top) and American astronaut Thomas P. Stafford met in space when their Apollo and Soyuz capsules were joined in orbit.

A spacecraft that could carry people had to protect against radiation and heat.

When a spacecraft reenters Earth's atmosphere, the outside of the craft grows red hot. This heat is caused by friction between the spacecraft and gases in the atmosphere. A heat shield was invented to

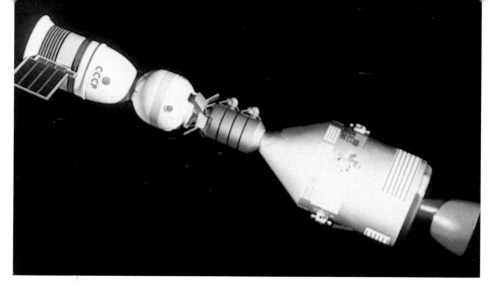

America's Apollo spacecraft (right) docked
with a Soviet Soyuz spacecraft in 1975.

keep the spacecraft and
the people inside from
burning up.

The Soviets and the
Americans built spacecraft
for carrying people into
space. The Soviets trained to
fly in space are called
cosmonauts. The Americans
are called astronauts.

Cosmonaut Yuri Gagarin (left) became the first person in space when the *Vostok 1* (right) was launched in 1961.

THE FIRST HUMANS IN SPACE

The first person to fly into space was a Soviet cosmonaut named Yuri Gagarin. He was carried in a spacecraft called *Vostok 1* on April 12, 1961.

The first American to fly

Astronauts
Alan B. Shepard, Jr.,
(left) and John H.
Glenn, Jr. (right)

into space was astronaut
Alan B. Shepard, Jr. His
spacecraft was called
Freedom 7. It was launched
on May 5, 1961.

The first American to orbit
Earth was John H. Glenn, Jr.
His spacecraft, called
Friendship 7, was launched
on February 20, 1962.

SPACE CAPSULES

The first spacecraft to carry people were called capsules. The first American space capsules were developed for a program called Project Mercury. Only one person could squeeze into a Mercury space capsule.

Astronauts in Mercury space capsules had very little control over their craft. And they could not stay in orbit much longer than one day.

Freedom 7 ready for launching at Cape Canaveral, Florida

An American Gemini capsule (left) and a Soviet Soyuz capsule (right) in orbit

The next type of American space capsule was called Gemini.

The first Soviet space capsule was called Vostok. The Soviets used space capsules called Soyuz into the 1990s.

A Saturn V rocket lifts *Apollo 8* off its launch pad.
The *Apollo 8* astronauts orbited the Moon but did not land.

GOING TO THE MOON

In the late 1960s, the United States built a spacecraft that could carry people to the Moon. This type of craft was called Apollo. It was launched by a huge rocket called the Saturn V.

The Apollo spacecraft also carried a small landing craft called the lunar module for taking astronauts from the

The *Apollo 11* lunar module, *Eagle*, over the Moon

spacecraft down to the surface of the Moon.

Apollo 11, launched on July 16, 1969, carried the first human beings to the Moon. The first person to set foot on the Moon was astronaut Neil A. Armstrong.

The lift-off of the Apollo 11 Moon mission

Neil Armstrong photographed Edwin Aldrin stepping down from the lunar module. Millions of people all over the world read about the landing.

On July 20, 1969, he and Edwin E. Aldrin, Jr., landed on the Moon.

Five other Apollo spacecraft landed on the Moon. The last Apollo flight to the Moon, *Apollo 17*, was launched on December 7, 1972.

BUILDING REUSABLE SPACECRAFT

The early spacecraft that carried people could only be used once. The Mercury, Gemini, and Apollo spacecraft all returned to Earth by parachuting into the sea.

American space capsules returned to Earth by parachuting into the sea (left), and the astronauts were recovered by the U.S. Navy (right).

These spacecraft were
very expensive to build.
So scientists wanted a
spacecraft that could be
used over and over again.

They designed the U.S.
Space Shuttle, the world's
first reusable spacecraft.

The Space Shuttle has
several parts. The astronauts
and their cargo ride in the
orbiter. The orbiter looks like
an airplane. When it returns
to Earth, it lands on a
runway.

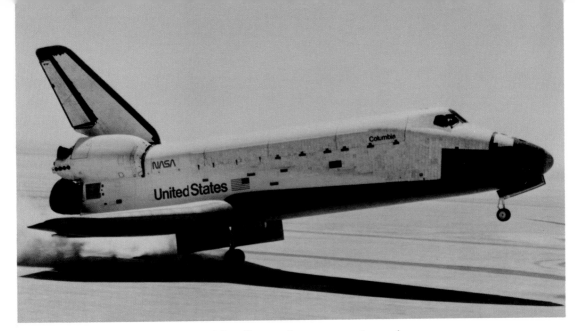

The Space Shuttle lands like a glider. Its engines are not used.

The orbiter is carried into space by rocket power. This power comes from the main engines on the orbiter and from two booster rockets that are strapped to a gigantic main fuel tank. After launch, the booster rockets and the fuel tank drop into the sea. The booster rockets are picked up by ships and used again.

The first shuttle flights into space were made by the orbiter *Columbia*, beginning in 1981.

The Space Shuttle *Columbia* lifting off on its second space mission in November 1981.

PEOPLE ON THE SHUTTLE

Some of the Space Shuttle astronauts are scientists and some are pilots. The scientists are called mission specialists and payload specialists. They launch satellites and perform experiments in space.

After the shuttles had made 24 flights, a great tragedy happened. During the 25th launch, on January 28, 1986, the Space Shuttle *Challenger* exploded. All

The *Challenger* crew: Front row (left to right), Michael J. Smith, Francis R. Scobbe, Ronald E. McNair. Back row (left to right), Ellison S. Onizuka, Christa McAuliffe, Gregory B. Jarvis, Judith A. Resnik.

seven people aboard, including a schoolteacher and observer, Christa McAuliffe, were killed.

The accident was caused by a leak in one of the booster rockets. The rockets had to be redesigned, and shuttles did not fly again until 1988.

Meanwhile, the Soviet Union also built a shuttle. It was test-flown in 1988.

The Soviet space shuttle is called *Buran*, which means "snowstorm."

INTERPLANETARY SPACECRAFT

Robot spacecraft are used to explore the planets and the regions of outer space. Interplanetary spacecraft receive the power for their journey from the Sun. They convert sunlight into electricity in solar panels that spread out from the craft like wings.

They carry cameras and scientific instruments to examine the planets and

The painting at left shows a satellite as it studies Earth's oceans from orbit. A solar panel (right) on a spacecraft converts the Sun's energy into electric power to run the onboard systems.

their moons. Radios beam the pictures and other information back to Earth.

Interplanetary spacecraft have explored Mars, Venus, and Mercury. Spacecraft have also visited Jupiter, Saturn, Uranus, and Neptune.

The painting above shows *Voyager 2* passing by Uranus. *Voyager 2* photographed Uranus (inset below) and Neptune (below). The white spot is a high-altitude cloud.

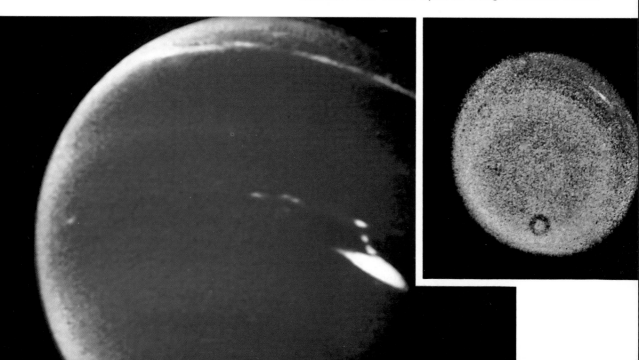

Pioneer 10 was launched on March 3, 1972.
It has now traveled beyond our solar system.

The first spacecraft to leave our solar system was called *Pioneer 10*. It entered the space between the stars in 1983. It carries a plaque with information about Earth in case intelligent beings someday find the spacecraft.

SATELLITES

While spacecraft were being used to explore the Moon and the planets, other spacecraft were used to help people on Earth. These spacecraft are called satellites. They orbit Earth.

Some of them swoop around our planet. Some of them orbit so that they always stay above the same spot on Earth.

A communications satellite is launched from the Space Shuttle.

The Space Shuttle can launch satellites (left) and retrieve them for repairs. The Hubble Space Telescope (right) was launched from the shuttle's cargo bay.

There are satellites that transmit telephone calls and TV pictures. These are called communications satellites.

There are satellites that scientists use to study the ocean, the atmosphere,

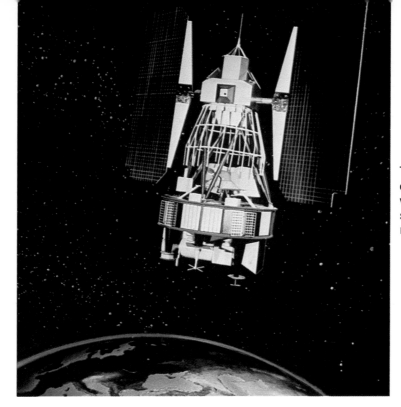

This satellite, called *Landsat*, was designed to study Earth's natural resources.

weather patterns, and
features on the land. These
are called scientific satellites.

There are satellites that
carry telescopes into orbit
above Earth's atmosphere.
Up high, the telescopes can
see better into deep space. **39**

SPACE STATIONS

Soviet cosmonauts
Leonid Jizim (right)
and Vladimir Solovev

Spacecraft that people can live and work on while in orbit are called space stations.

Nine small space stations have been put in orbit around Earth. Eight of these were built by the Soviet Union.

Cosmonauts went to and from these space stations in

The Soviet Soyuz spacecraft. Two solar panels
protrude from the sides of the capsule.

Soyuz space capsules. The space capsules docked with the space stations and the cosmonauts got on or off.

Some cosmonauts stayed in space stations for very long periods of time. The first stay of more than a year was a 366-day mission that ended in 1988.

The astronauts who orbited in *Skylab* performed experiments to study Earth and the Sun.

The United States only built one space station, called *Skylab*. It was launched in 1973. Three crews of astronauts rode up to *Skylab* and back in Apollo spacecraft.

Skylab fell from orbit in 1979. It burned up when it reentered Earth's atmosphere.

FUTURE SPACECRAFT

The United States wants to build a permanent space station. It would be built in orbit from materials carried up by the Space Shuttle.

Aboard the space station, people would build things and make chemicals that cannot be made in Earth's gravity. Scientists would carry out experiments in the weightlessness of space.

Future spacecraft with artificial gravity may carry

A space shuttle on its way to a space colony might dock at a space station to drop off supplies.

people to distant planets, such as Mars.

But a permanent space station or a manned Mars mission would be very expensive. Some experts wonder whether such projects are worth the cost.

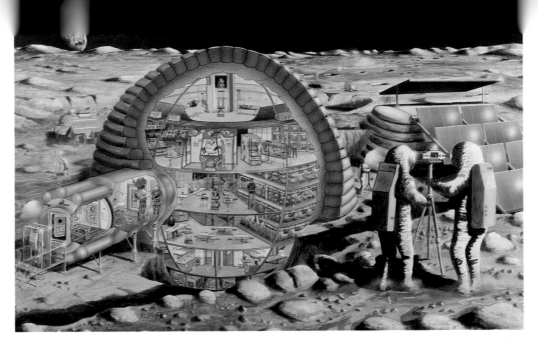

This drawing shows what a space colony on the Moon might look like.

Other experts say that many nations could cooperate in building a space station. And if people learn to live and work in the space around Earth, they may learn how to someday live in colonies on the Moon or even on Mars.

WORDS YOU SHOULD KNOW

artificial (AR • tih • FISH • il) — made by people; not natural

astronaut (AST • roh • nawt) — the American term for a person trained to fly in space

atmosphere (AT • muss • feer) — the layer of gases that surrounds Earth and some other planets

booster (BOO • stir) — something that gives extra lift or power

capsule (KAP • sil) — the enclosed part of a spacecraft that carries the astronauts, instruments, etc.

colonies (KAH • luh • neez) — settlements made by people who leave their own land or planet to live in another land or planet

combustion chamber (kum • BUSS • chin CHAYM • ber) — a closed-in space in which the burning of fuel takes place

communications (kuh • myoon • nih • KAY • shunz) — giving and receiving information

cosmonaut (KAHZ • muh • nawt) — the Soviet term for a person trained to fly into space

dock (DAHK) — to come together; to join with another craft

experiment (ex • PEHR • ih • mint) — the testing of a scientific idea to see if it is true

friction (FRIK • shun) — the rubbing of one thing against another;

gas (GASS) — a substance that is not solid or liquid, but flows freely and is able to expand indefinitely

gravity (GRAV • ih • tee) — the force that holds things down to a heavenly body or that pulls objects toward each other

instrument (IN • struh • mint) — a tool or a machine used for scientific work such as measuring or weighing

interplanetary (in • ter • PLAN • ih • tair • ee) — between the planets; from one planet to another

lunar (LOO • ner) — having to do with the Moon

module (MAHD • yool) — a self-contained unit that operates within a larger system

orbit (OR • bit) — to travel around an object in space; the path an object takes when it moves around another object

parachuting (PAIR • uh • SHOOT • ing) — lowering to Earth by means of a canopy of cloth that slows the fall

plaque (PLAK) — a thin plate of metal, plastic, etc., on which messages are written

pressure (PRESH • er) — the continued pushing action of a force

radiation (ray • dee • AY • shun) — light, heat, etc.; the rays given off by some substances because of changes inside them

robot (ROH • baht) — a machine that is made to imitate the actions of a human being; a machine that performs tasks when given commands

satellite (SAT • il • ite) — a body that revolves around a heavenly body; a moon is a natural satellite, while *Sputnik 1* was an artificial satellite

science fiction (SYE • ence FIK • shun) — made-up stories about space travel, future scientific developments, time travel, etc.

solar (SOH • ler) — having to do with the Sun

specialist (SPESH • ih • list) — a person who is specially qualified in some field of study

telescope (TEL • ih • skohp) — an instrument that makes distant objects look closer

weightlessness (WAYT • less • ness) — the condition experienced in Earth orbit when the speed of the spacecraft balances the pull of gravity so that people and objects float in space

INDEX

About the Author

Darlene R. Stille is a Chicago-based science writer and editor.